THE HUMAN
GENOME

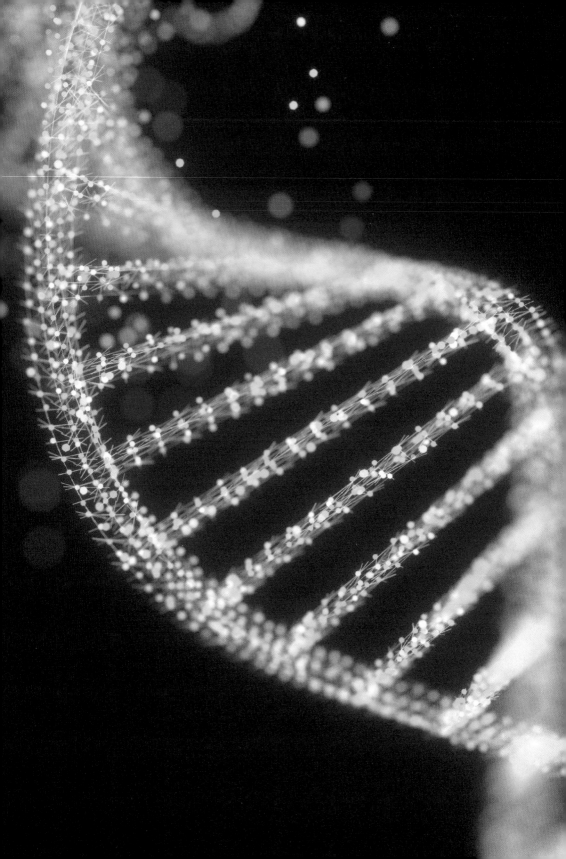

THE HUMAN GENOME

ODYSSEYS

JIM WHITING

CREATIVE EDUCATION · CREATIVE PAPERBACKS

Published by Creative Education and Creative Paperbacks
P.O. Box 227, Mankato, Minnesota 56002
Creative Education and Creative Paperbacks are imprints of
The Creative Company
www.thecreativecompany.us

Design and production by Blue Design (www.bluedes.com)
Art direction by Rita Marshall

Photographs by Getty (CNBC, JUAN GAERTNER/ SCIENCE, David S. Holloway,
PHOTO LIBRARY, KTSDESIGN/ SCIENCE PHOTO LIBRARY, Science & Society
Picture Library, Westend61/Andrew Brookes), iStock (Dr_Microbe, gevende,
Pgiam, sitox), Library of Congress (Romanov court photographer), MRC
Laboratory of Molecular Biology (Rosalind Franklin), NHGRI (Ernesto Del
Aguila III), National Cancer Institute (Eric Snyder), Unsplash (National Cancer
Institute) Wikimedia Commons (NIH, Wellcome Library, London)

Library of Congress Cataloging-in-Publication Data
Names: Whiting, Jim, 1943- author.
Title: The human genome / by Jim Whiting.
Description: Mankato, Minnesota : Creative Education and Creative
  Paperbacks, [2023] | Series: Odysseys in recent events | Includes
  bibliographical references and index. | Audience: Ages 12-15 | Audience:
  Grades 7-9 | Summary: "Teens explore the history of the Human Genome
  Project from a journalistic viewpoint to understand the events that made
  genome sequencing possible, the people involved, and its impact on the
  field of medicine"— Provided by publisher.
Identifiers: LCCN 2022015478 (print) | LCCN 2022015479 (ebook) | ISBN
  9781640267121 (library binding) | ISBN 9781682772683 (paperback) | ISBN
  9781640008533 (ebook)
Subjects: LCSH: Human genome—Juvenile literature.
Classification: LCC QH447 .W45 2023 (print) | LCC QH447 (ebook) | DDC
  611/.0181663—dc23/eng/20220611
LC record available at https://lccn.loc.gov/2022015478
LC ebook record available at https://lccn.loc.gov/2022015479

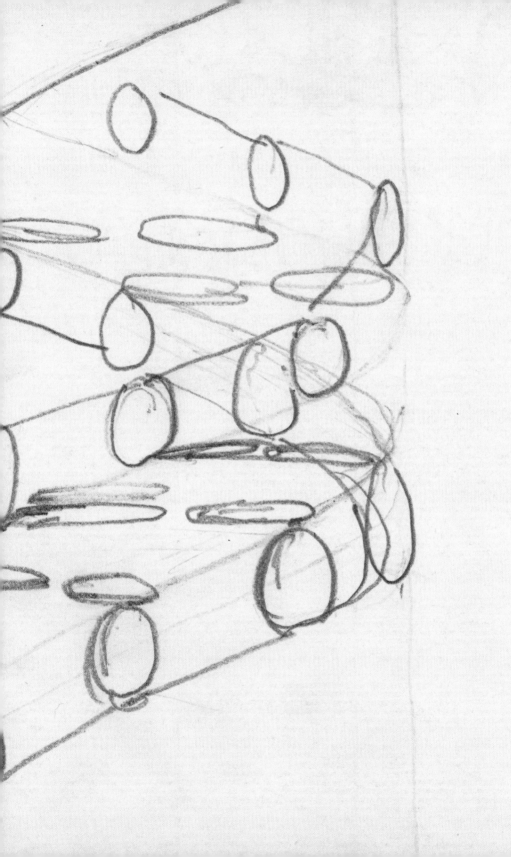

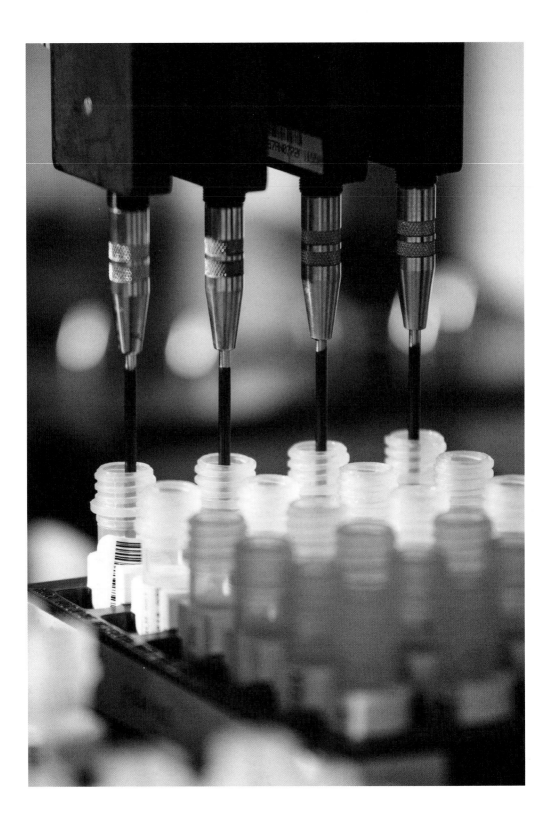

CONTENTS

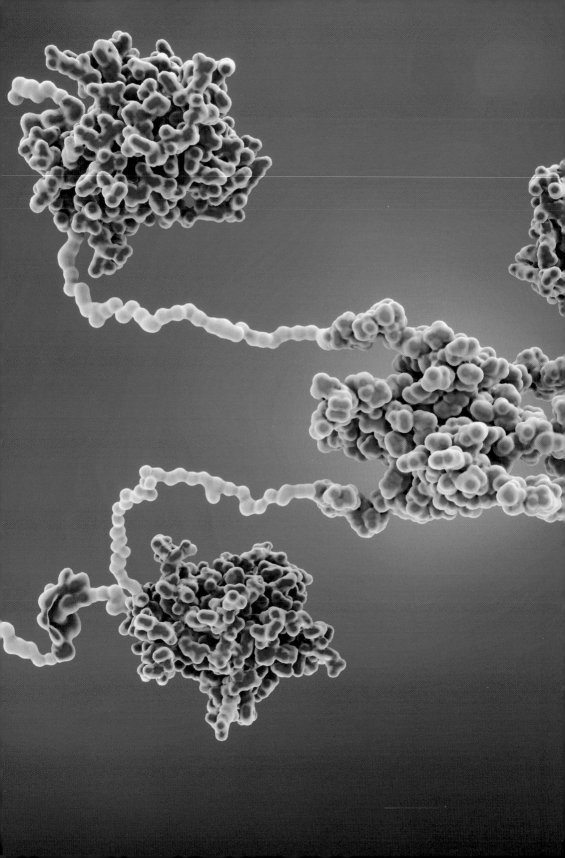

Introduction

Many people call the **sequencing** of the human **genome** through the Human Genome Project (HGP) the first great scientific achievement of the 21st century. Described in its simplest form, the human genome is the total genetic makeup of a human being. Genetic material is based on genes. Genes are the "codes" that determine your physical characteristics, such as hair and eye color.

OPPOSITE: Thousands of genes on a given chromosome are responsible for providing instructions that make proteins, such as the gene TP53 and its tumor-suppressing protein *(pictured)*.

All genes contain deoxyribonucleic acid (DNA). Unless you have an identical twin, your DNA is unique. So is your genome.

The HGP officially began its work in 1990. Scientists from many different countries took part. The project concluded in 2003, two years earlier than originally planned. Thanks to advancements in computer technology, scientists were able to move more quickly than expected through the genome. A rivalry between two groups of scientists also spurred competition.

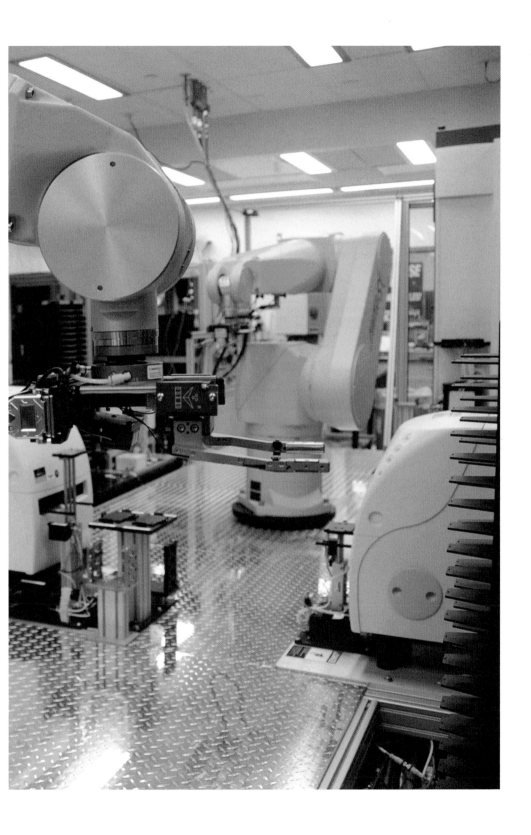

DNA samples collected at a crime scene may help forensic scientists target suspects.

The project has had many benefits. For instance, advances in health care now allow for earlier detection and treatment of serious diseases. There are even applications beyond medicine—in the criminal justice field! These advances and others are why the HGP has been called a turning point in world history.

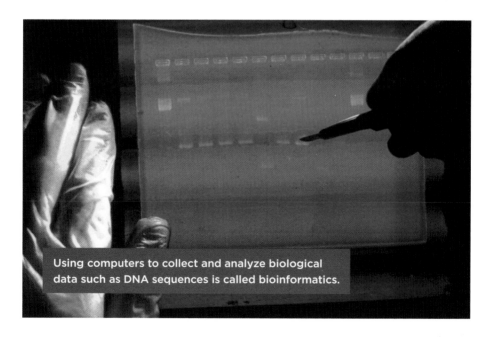

Using computers to collect and analyze biological data such as DNA sequences is called bioinformatics.

Secret of Life

The roots of the HGP were laid down in the mid-1850s in the garden of a **monastery** in Brno, a city near Prague, Czech Republic. For a long time, people had wondered about the principles of heredity. For example, why would a brother and sister with the same parents have different-colored eyes and hair? A monk named Gregor Mendel decided to answer that question and many others about the way in which one generation passes along its characteristics to the next.

OPPOSITE: By studying peas, Mendel was able to effectively limit the number of variables, or aspects that changed from one phase to the next, and better predict the outcomes.

Pea plants have seven characteristics with only two contrasting forms, which is why Mendel chose them.

Mendel used the pea plants in the monastery's garden for his study. Pea plants have seven characteristics with only two contrasting forms, which is why Mendel chose them. He called these characteristics factors. They included the height of the plant (tall or short), the texture of the peas (smooth or wrinkled), pea color (yellow or green), flower color (white or purple), flower position (at the tip of the plant or along the side), pod color (green or yellow), and shape of the pod (fully inflated or constricted). He wanted to see if he could discover a pattern among these factors in successive generations.

Mendel began his experiments with a parent generation, which he called P. He bred it and called the next generation F_1. All the F_1 plants displayed the same factors. They were tall. Their flowers were all purple. The peas themselves were all smooth. Things got interesting with the next generation, called F_2. About one-fourth of the plants were short, even though their parents were both tall. The same proportions held true for smooth and wrinkled peas, white and purple flowers, and the other four factors. Mendel called factors such as tall, smooth, and purple "dominant." They would always hide the other, "recessive" factor. But the short, wrinkled, and white factors did not disappear from the peas' DNA. If a recessive factor appeared in two parent plants, their offspring might display it. Many years later, British biologist Reginald Punnett made a diagram to show the relationship between dominant and recessive characteristics. It reveals why about one-fourth of members of succeeding generations display recessive characteristics.

Mendel worked with his pea plants for nearly 10 years. He published his findings in a relatively obscure science journal in 1866. His work received little attention—perhaps thanks, in part, to all the mathematical formulas included. Biologists of

Gregor Mendel

Gregor Mendel grew up on a farm. He was a good student who wanted to attend the best schools in the region. But his family couldn't afford it. He joined a monastery instead. The leader of the monastery sent Mendel to the University of Vienna. That allowed him to learn as much as possible about math and science, his favorite subjects. When he returned to the monastery, he began teaching at a local school. But Mendel wanted to make a name for himself. He began his studies with pea plants. In later life, he became the head of his monastery.

Johann Friedrich Miescher

that era seldom delved into mathematics. After years of neglect, Mendel's work was rediscovered in 1900. Several scientists, working independently, confirmed what Mendel had written. Today, he is known as the "father of genetics."

By then, other scientists had made related and important discoveries. Just three years after Mendel published his paper, Swiss biochemist Johann Friedrich Miescher made a startling discovery. His subject was far different from Mendel's peas. Miescher collected discarded, pus-filled bandages from patients with serious infections. Washing off the pus, he was able to study lymphoid (white blood) cells. He found a large, previously unknown molecule in the nucleus, or center, of the white blood cells. Because of its location in the nucleus, Miescher named it nuclein. Soon afterward, it became known as nucleic acid. Eventually it would acquire its full name of deoxyribonucleic acid, or DNA. Miescher was able to tell that it was made up of the elements hydrogen, oxygen, phosphorus, and nitrogen. He had no idea that his nuclein had any connection with heredity. In fact, for several decades, no one realized it.

Spurred in part by the renewed interest in Mendel's research, scientists at the start of the 20th century produced significant findings in the principles of heredity. They were especially interested in the composition and structure of the substance that actually transmitted characteristics from one generation to the next. Better microscopes enabled them to see into cellular structures. They discovered chromosomes, which consist of smaller units, called genes.

Chromosomes are made of DNA and proteins. Researchers found that DNA was composed of few chemicals. Protein appeared to be much more complicated than DNA. One researcher supposedly even called DNA "a stupid molecule." It seemed unlikely that it could contain all the information necessary to produce complex organisms. Therefore, scientists believed that proteins were the vehicles of heredity. But in the early 1940s, a team led by bacteriologist Oswald Avery proved that DNA was the way in which traits passed from one generation to the next.

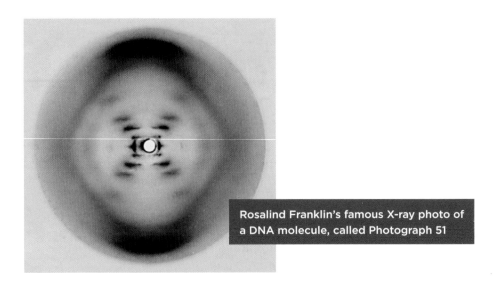

Rosalind Franklin's famous X-ray photo of a DNA molecule, called Photograph 51

Avery's team did not know what DNA looked like, though. Without that knowledge, they couldn't tell exactly *how* traits were passed along. Many scientists began working on this problem. In 1952, Rosalind Franklin took an X-ray photograph of a DNA molecule. The molecule looked like the letter X. This indicated it had the structure of a helix.

Physicist Maurice Wilkins showed Franklin's photo to British biologist Francis Crick and his American colleague James Watson. "The instant I saw the picture, my mouth fell open, and my pulse began to race," Watson said later. After studying the photo, he

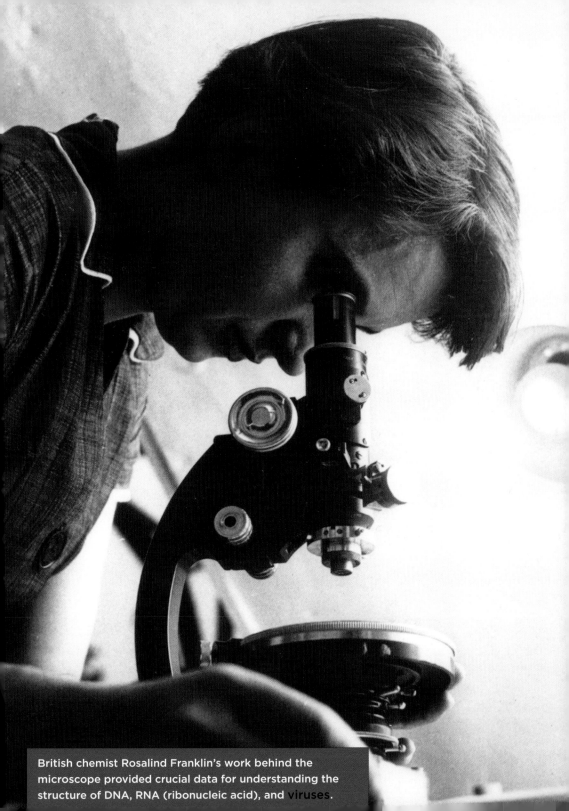

British chemist Rosalind Franklin's work behind the microscope provided crucial data for understanding the structure of DNA, RNA (ribonucleic acid), and viruses.

Boy or Girl?

Almost every cell in the human body has 46 chromosomes. They are arranged in pairs. However, egg and sperm cells have just 23 chromosomes. When a sperm cell unites with an egg, the two sets of chromosomes come together to form a single cell. It now has 46 chromosomes, in pairs. It eventually becomes a baby. The father determines the sex of the child. The mother's eggs all have an X chromosome. The father's sperm might have either an X or a Y. If the father provides an X chromosome, the result is typically an anatomically female baby. If it is a Y chromosome, the baby will have male anatomy.

and Crick determined that DNA has a double helix structure. It is like a spiraling ladder. The long sides consist of sugar and phosphate molecules that alternate with each other. The "rungs" are a series of four nitrogen-containing bases that are attached to each other, with a hydrogen **atom** in the center. One base is adenine, often called A for short. The others are thymine (T), guanine (G), and cytosine (C). In a DNA molecule, A and T always link up with each other in what are called base pairs. The same is true for G and C. The order of the bases determines the type of "instructions" contained in a DNA strand. Because of its ladder-like structure, DNA is able to replicate, or copy, itself when cells divide.

If a DNA molecule were fully unwound, it would stretch for about 6 feet (1.8 m). If all the DNA in the

"Gentlemen," [Crick] announced, "Watson and I have just discovered the secret of life!"

trillions of cells of the human body were linked, they would stretch to the sun and back at least 60 times. Yet DNA is so slender that thousands would fit through the eye of a needle.

Crick announced the discovery of this structure in a novel way. On February 28, 1953, he walked into a bar in Cambridge, England. (Crick, Watson, and many other noted scientists did their research at the University of Cambridge.) "Gentlemen," he announced, "Watson and I have just discovered the secret of life!" While their findings weren't initially accepted, in 1962, along with Wilkins, they won the Nobel Prize in Physiology or Medicine for their discovery.

James Watson *(left)* and Francis Crick *(right)* built upon the discoveries of others to conceptualize a model of DNA that showed how all the experimental data fit together.

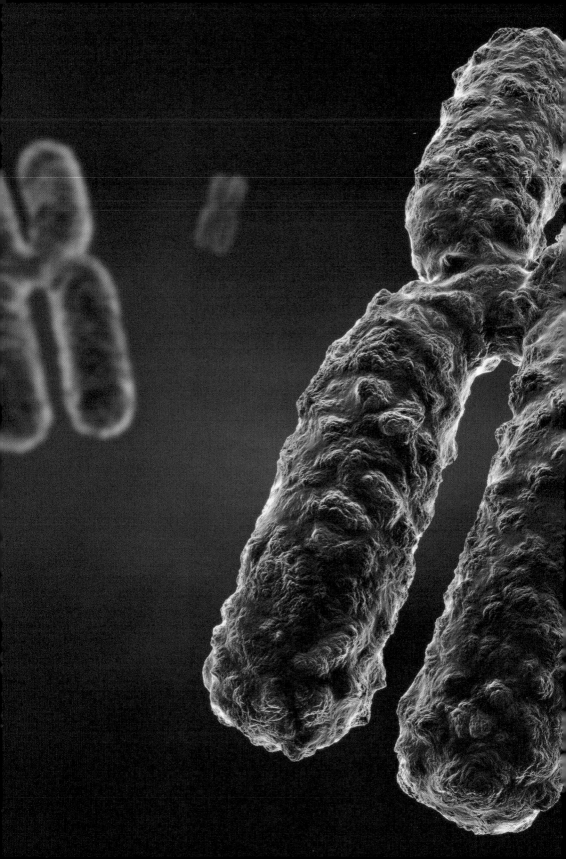

Thinking Big

The work of Watson and Crick firmly established the structure of DNA as it related to individual chromosomes and genes. A human DNA molecule consisted of 46 chromosomes. Each parent contributed half, or 23. Twenty-two of those pairs were basically the same. They shared traits such as eye and hair color with the corresponding chromosome from the other parent.

OPPOSITE: All chromosomal structures are said to have two sections called "arms."

The final one—the X or Y chromosome—was believed to determine an individual's sex.

But no one knew how many genes those 46 chromosomes contained. Genes aren't distributed evenly among chromosomes. Some chromosomes contain more than 3,000 genes, while others carry just a few hundred.

The next logical steps were to determine how many genes were in these chromosomes and where they were located within the individual chromosomes. A DNA molecule contained more than three billion individual base pairs. Figuring out their exact sequence would be a task of staggering complexity.

The term for the entire set of genes in a living organism dates back to 1920. German botanist Hans Winkler coined the term "genome," a word combining *gene* and *chromosome*. It refers to the entire set of genes in a living organism.

Yet it took time for the term and the underlying concept to gain widespread scientific acceptance. Watson and Crick helped, by heightening interest. As a result, geneticists began thinking about the sequence of the human genome, or the order in which genes appear along the DNA strands. Knowing the sequence would help them understand how traits are passed on and how human bodies function. It could also help physicians and

Computer-generated genetic sequence strips are written in a "language" of light and dark bands.

researchers gain a better understanding for diagnosing and treating—perhaps even preventing—many diseases.

At least there was a primitive model to follow. In the early 20th century, researcher Thomas Hunt Morgan studied the genes of fruit flies. The short lives of the insects made it easy to chart them over the course of many generations. In 1913, Morgan's assistant Alfred Sturtevant created the first-ever genetic map from the study of fruit flies. Morgan called Sturtevant's creation "one of the most amazing developments in the whole history of biology." The map laid the foundation for stunning growth and development in genetics research.

In 1977, biochemist Fred Sanger developed a way of sequencing a virus. It was much smaller than the human genome. The process was expensive and cumbersome. It took nearly two years. In the early 1980s, the process was improved. It was then possible to pinpoint the location of many disease genes in the body.

In 1985, biologist Robert Sinsheimer, the chancellor of the University of California, Santa Cruz, convened a meeting of geneticists from all around the world. He wanted to discuss the possibility of sequencing the human genome. In effect, they would make a map of it, which would identify all the genes in the genome. "It had occurred to me to wonder . . . was there something we weren't doing in biology, because we didn't think in terms of big science?" Sinsheimer said. "It seemed so successful in other fields. We didn't need a big machine like an accelerator or like a telescope, but it did occur to me that maybe we could use a big database, like a database of genomes, and sequences of genomes." Sinsheimer's proposal didn't gain much traction at first. Most attendees felt that the technology to take on such a daunting project was too primitive. At that time, the Epstein-Barr virus was the longest gene sequence that had been read. It had 150,000 base pairs. That was just 1/20,000th of the base pairs of the human genome. The price tag was huge: several billion dollars. Many people thought the money could be better spent elsewhere.

However, the following year, Italian-born virologist and **Nobel laureate** Renato Dulbecco wrote an article in *Science* magazine that called for an international human genome project. "The sequence of the human DNA is the reality of our species, and everything that happens in the world depends on those sequences." He said that it would be especially useful in understanding the nature of cancer, thereby helping to find cures for the deadly disease.

Transgenic Animals

Some scientists work with transgenic animals. Transgenicism involves inserting genes from one species of animal into the genome of a different one. One example is inserting a human gene into sheep, goats, or cows. The resulting milk from these animals has a human protein. This "super-milk" can be given to human babies. Some transgenic animals seem more in the realm of science fiction. For example, in one experiment, a gene from a glowing jellyfish was added to mouse DNA. This resulted in mice that actually glowed in the dark.

Technology used in the 1980s, such as this DNA synthesizer, evolved and became much more sophisticated by the time the HGP ended.

At about the same time, the U.S. Department of Energy became involved through its Office of Health and Environmental Research. The proposal gained funding in 1987 for what was to be called the Human Genome Project. Soon, the National Institutes of Health (NIH) also got involved. Congress insisted that the NIH be in charge of coordinating HGP efforts. Everyone agreed that the project needed a leader with a strong reputation in the scientific community. The choice was obvious: James Watson. "My first reaction to the Human Genome Project was negative," he said. "Why do the human [genome] when we hadn't done the bacteria [genome]? It just seemed a big jump ahead and requiring more money than they were likely to get."

Watson was also keenly aware of the fear that many people had of genetic research. The most notorious example was the Nazi regime in Germany before and during World War II (1939–1945). Nazi scientists had made efforts to produce a "master race" of tall people with blond hair and blue eyes.

Yet Watson soon overcame his reservations. "I changed my mind pretty fast because these discussions, while they sort of started independent of human genetics, soon became entangled with it, and it was clear that we were going to get better genetic maps, and we were going to have better chances of isolating disease genes if

Real-Life Mutants

According to estimates, less than 2 percent of humans are redheads. Because they are so rare, some people call them "unicorns of the real world." Hair color is not all that sets them apart. Evidence suggests that redheads are more sensitive to changes in temperature. They appear to tolerate pain better. And they really are mutants. During work in genome sequencing in the 1990s, researchers discovered that gene MC1R produces a substance called **melanin**. It determines hair and skin color. But sometimes this gene is mutated. It produces pheomelanin instead. That results in red hair. It can also account for lighter skin and freckles.

we went for the Human Genome Project." He became head of the HGP. Several other countries also joined. The project had become truly international in scope.

By 1989, the National Center for Human Genome Research had begun operations. Scientists were also sequencing simpler genomes, such as bacteria and mice. Their findings would help with the HGP. Still, it was a slow, painstaking process. First they had to map the locations of the chromosomes. Then they could begin sequencing individual genes. The project officially kicked off in 1990.

DYS	DYS	DYS	DYS	DYS	DYS	DYS
89II	390	391	392	393	426	438
15	19	14		16	13	1

Race to the Swift

As the HGP got underway, its sequencing methods proved to be somewhat laborious. This ensured accuracy, but some people were upset with the pace. Research was also spread amongst many university labs, with each lab responsible for different subsets of analysis. The workload was not concentrated in any one place.

OPPOSITE: DYS numbers show where sets of DNA molecules repeat on the Y chromosome. The markers often aid in forensics and paternity testing.

Biochemist Steven McKnight commented, "It's just a disaster. There is no cohesion, no focus, no game plan. To me, it's typical government work."

HGP scientist Craig Venter developed an alternative method. Using expressed sequence tags (EST), he claimed, would be much cheaper and faster. EST involved dividing DNA molecules into thousands of fragments. Then researchers would look for places at either end where the base pairs overlapped and reconnect them using a high-powered computer. Unquestionably

Swimming to Success

As a youth, Craig Venter didn't take his education seriously. He preferred to be on the water—swimming, sailing, and surfing. He joined the U.S. Navy during the Vietnam War (1954–1975). He worked in the intensive care ward of a field hospital. He was depressed by how many people he tried to help who were dying. One day he swam out into the ocean, intending to commit suicide. But he changed his mind. He devoted his life to medical research. "A doctor can save maybe a few hundred lives in a lifetime," he said. "A researcher can save the whole world." In 2007 and 2008, *TIME* magazine named him among the 100 Most Influential People in the World. He received a 2008 National Medal of Science from President Barack Obama.

it was faster and cheaper. But many scientists claimed it was too sloppy and incomplete. What if some fragments didn't overlap with anything else?

In 1992, Venter left the HGP. He founded the nonprofit The Institute for Genomic Research (TIGR). Pronounced "tiger," it reflected Venter's hard-charging personality. Not surprisingly, many other scientists were upset with him. He soon acquired the nickname "Darth Venter." TIGR had its first big success in 1995. Under Venter's direction, they completed sequencing the genome of the bacteria *Haemophilus influenzae*. It can cause pneumonia and meningitis. Lucy Shapiro of Stanford University noted the significance of it being "the first glimpse at the complete gene content of a living species."

More than three years later, the HGP finished sequencing the genome of a roundworm. It was the organization's first completed animal genome. Meanwhile, it had sequenced just 3 percent of the human genome. That same year, Venter started a new company called Celera. In Latin, *celer* means "swift." It reflected his desire to speed up the process even more. The company's motto was "Speed matters—discovery can't wait."

The following year, Venter passed the one billion mark of sequenced base pairs. So did the HGP. Then, knowing that the HGP's deadline was 2005, Venter pledged to finish sequencing by 2001. (The HGP then moved

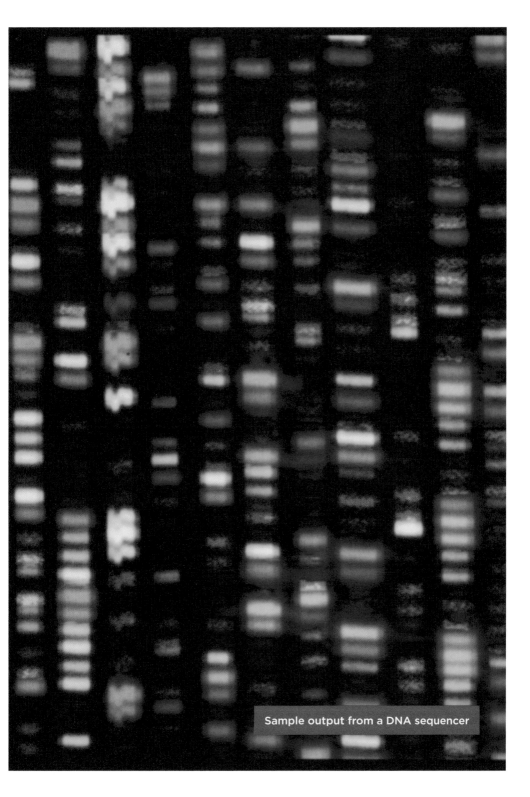

Sample output from a DNA sequencer

up its timeline to 2003.) Early in 2000, Venter said he had passed the 2.5 billion mark. The HGP reached two billion soon afterward. Venter continued upping the ante, claiming on April 6, 2000, that his company had completed sequencing almost the entire genome.

Such a rivalry did not soothe the ill feelings between Venter and the HGP. "More and more, the Human Genome Project, supposedly one of mankind's noblest undertakings, is resembling a mud-wrestling match," wrote Justin Gillis of the *Washington Post.* "The ongoing fight threatens to undermine confidence in the accuracy of gene maps that will be produced later this year. Those maps promise to hasten medical progress and offer profound insights into human biology."

On June 26, 2000, U.S. president Bill Clinton announced the completion of the first map of the human genome. "With this profound new knowledge," he said, "humankind is on the verge of gaining immense, new power to heal. Genome science will have a real impact on all our lives—and even more, on the lives of our children," Clinton added. "It will revolutionize the diagnosis, prevention, and treatment of most, if not all, human diseases."

Venter and HGP leader Francis Collins, who had replaced Watson several years earlier, put aside their differences long enough to flank the president on the stage. *New York Times* reporter Nicholas Wade summarized those differences: "Without Celera's challenge, the [HGP] would have had little reason to alter its academic flight path and produce the useful part of the genome three years ahead of the 2003 landing date. Without the HGP's challenge, Celera could be

"Humankind is on the verge of gaining immense, new power to heal. Genome science will have a real impact on all our lives—and even more, on the lives of our children."

commanding top dollar for its database, knowing its customers had no alternative."

The following year, both Celera and the HGP published their findings in respected scientific journals. Collins noted that the genome could be thought of in terms of a book with multiple uses: "It's a history book—a narrative of the journey of our species through time. It's a shop manual, with an incredibly detailed blueprint for building every human cell. And it's a transformative textbook of medicine, with insights that will give health care providers immense new powers to treat, prevent, and cure disease."

By May 2003, the HGP completed its work. The project had sequenced more than 3 billion base pairs, about 92 percent of the whole human genome. This included mapping more than 20,000 genes, with the anticipation that more would be discovered in the succeeding years as technology improved. Its findings went into a computer data bank. The ending of the HGP was the start of something else. As scientist and science writer Adam Rutherford notes, just 15 years after the genome was completed, science was able to extract an enormous amount of data from a person's genome. "And it's not limited to the rigor of formal science or governmental medical policy," he wrote. "You can spit in a test tube and get a readout of key parts of your own genome from an armada of companies that will tell you all sorts of

Jurassic Future?

Moviegoers have been thrilled by the dinosaurs in the *Jurassic Park* and *Jurassic World* movies. In the films, scientists extract dinosaur DNA from amber that is millions of years old to create the creatures. In the real world, that process is highly improbable. In 2013, researchers were unable to extract enough DNA from amber-coated flies that died more than 10,000 years ago to reconstruct even a single gene. As researcher Dr. David Penney said, "The Jurassic Park scenario must remain in the realms of fiction." He gave himself some wiggle room, though. "Never say never," he continued. "Technology and science have progressed so much that it may happen one day."

things about your characteristics, history, and risk of some diseases, for just a couple of hundred dollars."

Researchers continued sequencing the human genome years after the HGP ended to fill in the gaps of the genetic code. New technology enabled scientists to read long stretches of repeated DNA that used to be indiscernible. Now they could determine where those repeated sequences belonged in the genome. In 2022, a global team of more than 100 scientists called the Telomere-to-Telomere Consortium announced the full, end-to-end completion of the human genome. They sequenced 200 million new base pairs to fill in the remaining 8 percent of the code. The completed genome opens new opportunities for research in genetic variants that cause diseases and cancer, as well as shedding light on how certain traits have evolved in humans.

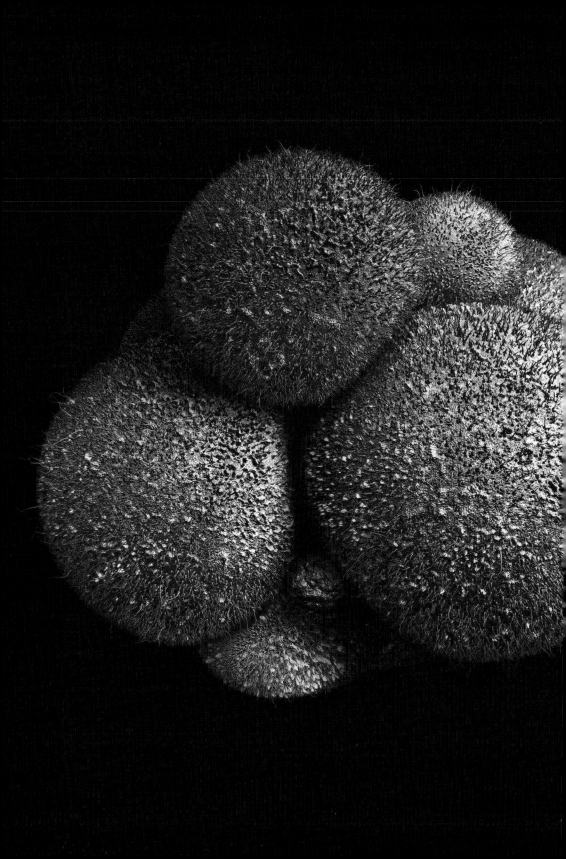

Value of the HGP

Even though the HGP officially ended in 2003, its effects continue. The greatest advance because of the HGP in the field of medicine involves the study and treatment of cancer. "Cancers arise when cells accumulate some combination of genetic events that serve as 'drivers' so that cell division outpaces cell death," said cancer geneticist Bert Vogelstein. Begun in 2006, the Cancer Genome Atlas project profiles the causes of cancer using genome sequencing.

OPPOSITE: Mitosis is the process of cellular division in which one cell divides into two identical ones, each having the same kind and number of chromosomes.

The BabySeq Project began in 2015. It tests the genomes of newborns for genetic defects. One family found that their daughter had a biotinidase deficiency. This prevented her body from using biotin, a vitamin that helps convert food into energy. In extreme cases, biotinidase deficiency can cause blindness, deafness, and seizures. Because the little girl had a mild version, conventional testing didn't reveal it. This early detection enabled the parents to confront the situation proactively. Robert Green, who heads the project, believes that the project will expand and result in vastly improved preventive care. "We want to move from a reactive health care system to a proactive health care system," he said.

According to the Centers for Disease Control and Prevention, hundreds of babies are born with some kind of genetic defect every day. A baby born to a family in Utah

Lung cancer *(in purple)* is often driven [by] the mutation of a gene called KRAS.

Guardian of the Genome

If genes assumed human form, number TP53 might wave a foam finger and chant, "I'm Number One!" It has been mentioned more than 8,500 times in upward of 40,000 scientific papers. That's nearly twice as often as any other gene. TP53 stops damaged cells from dividing. That helps prevent the formation of cancerous tumors. As a result, it is known as the "guardian of the genome." But if TP53 is mutated, or altered, it loses its tumor-fighting capability. That increases the likelihood of cancer. It's interesting to note that elephants have 20 TP53 genes. Humans have just one. As a result, elephants rarely get cancer.

GENETIC MAPPING
NHGRI FACT SHEETS
genome.gov

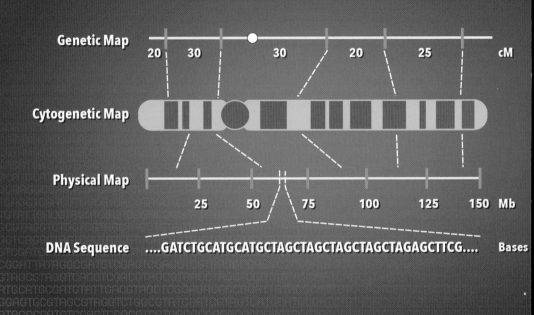

Genetic maps are tools scientists use to identify the genes responsible for disorders such as cancer, heart disease, and mental health conditions.

died suddenly at six months old. He had exceptionally large eyes and slightly wrinkled skin that gave him the appearance of an old man. Several other family members had also died from this mysterious disease. Using DNA sequencing, researchers found the defective gene in 16 months. "To be able to say, this kid is sick because of this, it's almost too real," said Mark Yandell, a scientist who played a key role in developing the computer program that enabled researchers to isolate the gene. Armed with this knowledge, the family could use in vitro fertilization to select embryos that didn't have this gene.

In 2018, researchers announced a powerful new test for determining inherited risks for heart disease, breast cancer, Type 2 diabetes, chronic inflammatory bowel disease, and atrial fibrillation. The test measures DNA changes in 6.6 million places in the human genome.

That is vastly more accurate than usual genetic tests. The test identifies at least 10 times more people who are susceptible to these diseases.

Another benefit of the HGP is new and better medications. Some of these drugs can be targeted at individuals based on their genomes. In the next decade, we may also be better able to determine which drugs work best for an individual, based on the person's genetic makeup.

The HGP has exerted a significant effect in fields beyond medicine. One notable example is in **forensics**. Crime scene investigators use DNA to identify suspects through tiny samples of hair, saliva from a drinking glass, or dried blood. The samples are analyzed using the Combined DNA Index System (CODIS), managed by the Federal Bureau of Investigation (FBI). Similarly, other countries' government agencies also log DNA samples from convicted criminals in "banks" to help identify future perpetrators. While politically controversial, such policy has proven effective. A repository of DNA evidence has also enabled innocent people to be cleared of unjust charges, sometimes decades later. About a quarter of exonerations happen as the result of DNA evidence.

An unusual case of DNA "fingerprinting" involved a woman named Anna Anderson. In 1918, Russian

Bolshevik revolutionaries murdered Czar Nicholas II, his wife, and their five children. Two years later, a woman named Anna Anderson claimed that she was actually Anastasia Romanov, the czar's youngest daughter, and had survived the slaughter. Claims and counterclaims went back and forth for many years. Most of the Russian royal family's remains were discovered in the early 1990s. DNA eventually confirmed that Anastasia had indeed perished along with the rest of her family. Anderson's story was bogus.

Genomic testing is so common today that it can be done from your own home. Biotechnology companies have taken the concept straight to consumers who want to know more about their DNA. Home delivery kits test a saliva sample in a lab where part of the genome is sequenced to look for mutations. Within a few weeks, an

Czar Nicholas II *(center)* and his immediate family, circa 1914

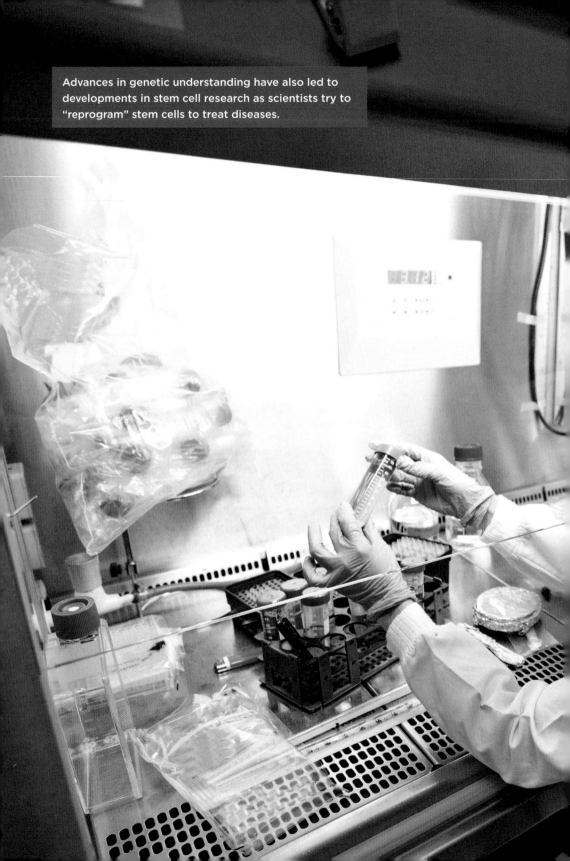

Advances in genetic understanding have also led to developments in stem cell research as scientists try to "reprogram" stem cells to treat diseases.

analysis shows a person's basic ancestry or **predispositions** to certain health conditions. The technology for whole genome sequencing has become so advanced and cost-effective that it is often used in research studies.

The HGP also transformed the rules of research and biological discovery. Despite the competition between Venter and the HGP leaders, the project as a whole was one of the largest collaborative biological undertakings in the world. While the project was unfolding, a digital revolution was also taking place. By 2000, the HGP was using computers to manage all the digital genome data and storing everything on an online database for anyone to use. To have all the information accessible at the click of a mouse was a game-changer. It created a new standard for data scaling, digitization, and sharing, which projects such as the Cancer Genome Atlas used to engage more scientists and civilians. "The real fruits of the HGP lie in the contrast between the primitive state of digital biology in the late 1980s and the current ease with which all scholars can access, harness, and analyze biological data," says geneticist Richard Gibbs, who founded the Human Genome Sequencing Center. He encourages new researchers to be as familiar with computer languages as they are with lab equipment because technology is becoming increasingly integral to biological discoveries.

According to the NIH, the complete sequence of the human genome is like having the complete manual to the human body. "The challenge now is to determine how to read the contents of these pages and understand how all of these many, complex parts work together in human health and disease," says the NIH. Genomic research is still in relative infancy. It is as if we are explorers who have just cast off our moorings and begun venturing into the open sea. We believe that what lies far beyond the horizon will change our world forever. But we can only guess about the nature of that future world—or the twists and turns we will have to take to reach it.

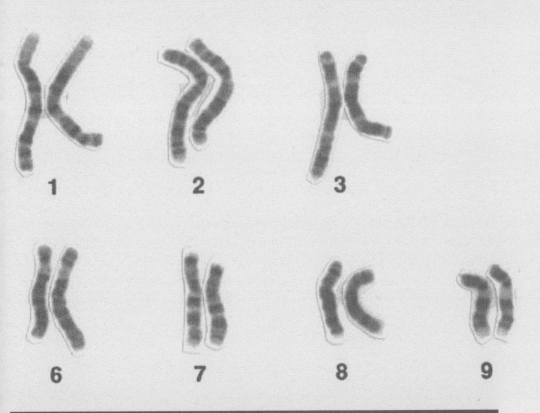

1 2 3

6 7 8 9

Bet on It

One of the HGP's main goals was to determine how many genes were packed into the 46 chromosomes. British geneticist Ewan Birney started a betting pool among his colleagues to guess the actual number. Originally it cost $1 to enter, then $5, and finally $20. A total of 460 people entered. Some had won Nobel Prizes. Most had one thing in common: Their bets were wildly wrong. Many guessed more than 100,000. The highest estimate was 291,059. The winner predicted 25,947. The exact number remains unknown. According to the National Human Genome Research Institute, it's about 30,000.

19 20

Selected Bibliography

Gibson, Greg. *It Takes a Genome: How a Clash Between Our Genes and Modern Life Is Making Us Sick*. Upper Saddle River, N.J.: FT Press Science, 2009.

Lipkin, Steven Monroe, and Jon R. Luoma. *The Age of Genomes: Tales from the Front Lines of Genetic Medicine*. Boston, Mass.: Beacon Press, 2016.

Mukherjee, Siddhartha. *The Gene: An Intimate History*. New York City, N.Y.: Scribner, 2016.

Rutherford, Adam. *A Brief History of Everyone Who Ever Lived: The Human Story Retold through Our Genes*. New York City, N.Y.: The Experiment, 2017.

Ryan, Frank. *The Mysterious World of the Human Genome*. Amherst, N.Y.: Prometheus Books, 2016.

Venter, J. Craig. *A Life Decoded: My Genome—My Life*. New York City, N.Y.: Viking, 2007.

Glossary

atom the smallest particle of a chemical element that can exist alone or in combination

bacterium a one-celled living organism without an organized nucleus; may be harmful (causing infection) or beneficial (fermentation of yogurt); the plural form is "bacteria"

biochemist a person who studies chemical reactions that take place in living organisms

chancellor a person in a position of high rank, especially at a university

forensics the use of scientific tests and techniques to solve crimes

geneticist a person who studies heredity and the variations of inherited characteristics

genome the complete set of nuclear DNA in an organism

helix a spiral object shaped like the threads on a screw or a winding staircase

in vitro fertilization fertilization of an egg performed or taking place in a test tube, culture dish, or elsewhere outside a living organism

melanin	dark pigment that occurs in the hair, eyes, and skin; this is responsible for skin tanning when exposed to sunlight
molecule	two or more atoms held together by a chemical bond
monastery	the site where a community of monks (men who have taken religious vows) lives and works
Nobel laureate	someone who has won a Nobel Prize
predisposition	the tendency to a condition or quality, usually based on the combined effects of genetic and environmental factors
sequencing	the process of discovering the order in which chemical substances are combined within DNA
virus	a submicroscopic agent that infects living things and consists of a single or double DNA strand

Websites

Nature | Human Genome Project—By the Numbers
https://www.nature.com/articles/d41586-021-00314-6
This article traces the effects the HGP has had on genomics
   since 2001.

Nemours TeensHealth | Genes and Genetics
https://kidshealth.org/en/teens/genes-genetic-disorders.html
Learn more about the basic principles of DNA and follow links
   to other aspects of genetics and heredity.

PBS | Biotechnology: Sequencing the Human Genome
(Retro Report)
https://tpt.pbslearningmedia.org/resource/biotechnology-
   sequencing-the-human-genome-video/retro-report/
Watch a video on the history of the HGP and learn about the
   complications in gene-based medicines.

YourGenome | What Is DNA?
https://www.yourgenome.org/facts/what-is-dna
Learn more about the basic principles of DNA.

Index